Unicorn Sprinkles

Jennifer Markham

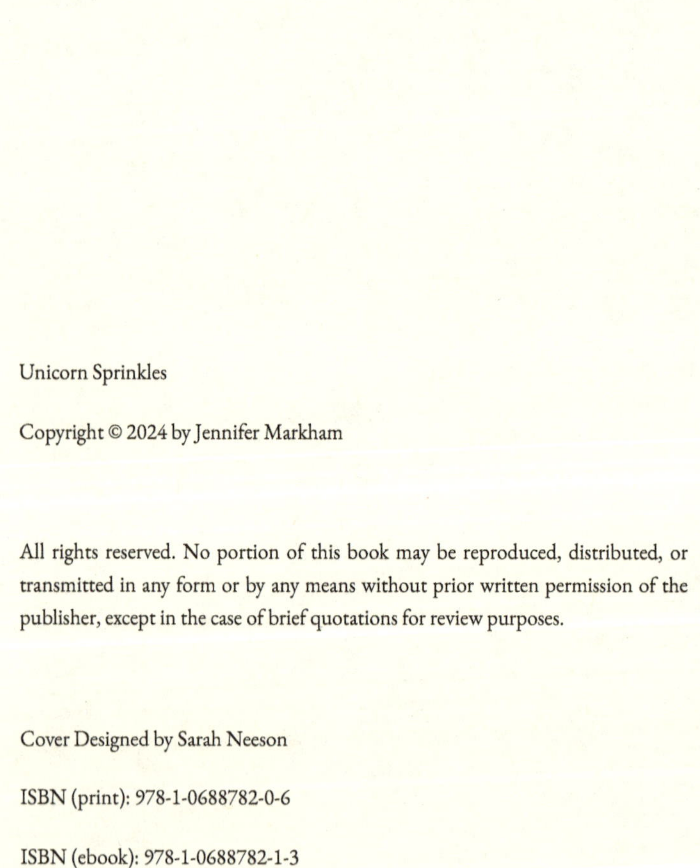

Unicorn Sprinkles

Cover Designed by Sarah Neeson

ISBN (print): 978-1-0688782-0-6

ISBN (ebook): 978-1-0688782-1-3

For Dad,

forever the best man I know

Contents

These two ducks

Relaxing, pluming each other.
With no body of water anywhere nearby.

Of course they are romantically involved,
they just wanted more privacy.
Maybe the other ducks didn't approve of the union.

These two ducks are oblivious
to the idea that they're out of place at all,
feathers fluffing about around them.

Don't tell them though,
unaware and in love is a way to be!

Even if you're a duck in a soccer field.

Colour me happy

I want to tie dye my life.

I'm pink,
the colour your sheepish cheeks go.
And the sky at sunset.

I'm blue,
da ba dee ah bah dye.
But not with sadness.

I'm green,
like the guys at the Canuck's games,
and happy grass.

I'm yellow,
but the sunshiny bright one,
not like mustard.

I'm purple,
oh how I'd so love to BE purple.
Royal and universally loved.

Put those gloves on,
grab the plastic bottles and dye
pitter patter, let's get at 'er.

Roly poly, Pumpki

You, little glittery Pumpki,
have had quite the adventure.

We don't hold it against you,
that you're made to light up,
but ran out of energy.

You do you Pumpki.

In the meantime, you just roll about,
exploring your surroundings.

Follow the road less rolled,
little glittery Pumpki.

My Rainbow

You bring happiness into my life
when I didn't think that was possible.

Midstorm, you show right up.

You make me so happy.
Let's be honest, everything is riding against
a long-term future.

But you don't seem to care about that.

You make me feel safe, comforted and loved.
You whirled into my life, full of colour and positivity,
and hug me like I'm about to float away.

I know you have your hang ups too,
but for now, this works.

Cheers to you, Rainbow.

Bridge birdies

Two birds sat together on the lamp standard,
with their backs to the camera,
looking out over the Lion's Gate Bridge.

Phil and Doug were likely discussing the weather,
or their latest garbage find, but they looked absolutely in love.

So much so, that I took a screenshot
for a Valentine's day post
at the very second when they glanced at each other.

Captured as a single moment,
they stared longingly into each other's eyes,
with the idyllic bridge as their backdrop.

Only a sunset could have made it more romantic,
as they discussed the stock market or housing crisis.

Steam swirls

The log cabin in Robert's Creek,
has a small hot water tank, but Diane,
bless her heart, boils me some on the stove.

Her oven mitts on either side
of the mashed potato pot, as she hurry-waddles
into the bathroom to dump it in.

Cranberry bubble bath,
and my hair cascading around me
like a wet veil hug.

The steam swirling up from the bubbles,
twirling in the sunlight streaming in
from the fogged glass window.

So peaceful,
I'm finally at ease.

Ladybug

Do you believe in reincarnation?
I think I do.

But let me say,
if I come back as something lame
like a ladybug
I'm going to be one pissed off ladybug!
I'll be tearing around with vengeance,
for no other reason than:
I'm a ladybug.

I'll be spiteful and angry.
I'll climb on people,
let the aphids sabotage gardens.

Do you think it's possible animals have us fooled?
Maybe they're higher thinking beings too!

That means all the angry and spiteful humans
are just reincarnated ladybugs,
who didn't want to come back as humans.

Fruity TV

Do you have an Apple TV?

Bahahahahahahhah
ahhahahahha
hahhahah

I asked the TV
I got free from Michelle's parents
basement. It only likes oranges.

I've also only ever turned it on maybe
five times. Three of those to play N64.

It's mostly decoration, Auntie.
Maybe I'll buy an apple to hang on it.
Sorry, oranges.

Salty escape

I loved the energy of the parade,
the yelling, the people, the stickers,
it was all so fulfilling and soulful.

Until suddenly it wasn't.
It was too loud, hot and crowded.

I turned around to the ocean,
and started running.

A beautiful sense of calm started within me
when the parade noise faded into the waves
and I pulled my shoes off to wade in.

I underestimate the soothing effect
of water on my body.

And my soul.

Rainbow pride

It's more than the colours
and corporate appearances.

It's more than religion
and political movements.

It's not that there's a higher abundance
of pride in people in our city today.
It's just that today they all feel comfortable
being who they truly are.

I hope one day we live in a world,
they can present as who they feel inside
all year long.

Double dipping

My sister and I started in the ocean,
at sunset. We swam, as we
talked about seaweed and jellyfish.
We went farther than the land jutted out,
so the sunset was in full view.
I laid on my back and floated.
The salty water on my lips.

Then we drove 5 minutes to the lake.
We stopped at a little library in between,
but no new to me books needed rescuing.

The sun was almost fully gone
when we submerged into the cold water
down makeshifts stone stairs.
I floated there too,
under the deep sky full of sparkly stars,
as she talked about lake monsters
tickling our feetsies.

We giggled like we didn't have kids, jobs, husbands
or responsibilities.
Just juvenile bliss,
fully present in the water together.

Tattoo

This scarred skin,
these etched words
are the mark of someone
who's hurting less.

This scarred skin,
these etched words
mean I still miss him like crazy,
most days.

This scarred skin,
these etched words
represent slowly moving forward
with a mended broken heart.

That broken heart was a testament of love.
As is this scarred skin,
with these etched words.
Permanent grief growth.

You're weird

Thank you,
for that compliment.

Thank you,
for seeing me as I am.
As someone who doesn't fit society's
expectations of me.

Thank you,
for acknowledging my experience.
I don't change myself to mold
perfectly inside the box,
but instead thrive outside of it.

Thank you,
for celebrating what make us unique,
different, and quirky instead of us
all trying to be the same.

Tree dream

The sun beams
were coming through the trees
hitting the dust we'd kicked up,
and landing on the ferns
that peppered the forest floor.

Shania Twain played in the car,
my hair still wet from the lake,
the light breeze cooling my sunscreen-soaked arms,
gritty with the sand.

I tried to catch a frog,
but the slimy bugger kept slipping
out of my hands. I could've kissed it!
My missed opportunity for a charming prince.
He wasn't in it for love, so he got out of here.

Doggy parking

The dog park by the lake,
has two little gated spaces
by the exit to the washrooms.

Perfect for dog parents who come alone,
with little four-legged furry creatures
who chose violence that morning.

Winnie doesn't like being left in the car,
or anywhere really—but she trots right in
and sits while I close the gate,
to wait impatiently and quietly for me.

Perfect little doggy parker,
no reverse stall or parallel needed.

Christmas song happy

Eggnog oat latte in hand,
browsing at Chapters together
with my closest friends
I was already overwhelmingly happy.

I heard my first Christmas song of the season
and I realized – it won't be the same this year,
but that doesn't mean it will be bad.

There's still so much potential for magic,
and I'll do everything I can,
to make it the best one yet.

Heartful

As you were walking away last night,
you stopped to draw a heart on my car window
with your finger.

Little did you know,
Neeners did the same thing last week,
on the other side.

The two of you quite literally,
surrounded me with affection,
on both sides.

Bonus sunset

When I woke up after my night shift,
I knew I needed two things to feed my soul:
my dog and a body of water.

We got to the park by the ocean,
right as the sun was setting across the bay.

All the other dogs we saw had coats on,
we left all ours at home though,
fur-mom fail.

She ran and frolicked about, loving it all.
Not sure which of us needed it more.

On my own, not alone

Last night I felt lonely,
but instead of letting it make me feel sad,
felt grateful.

Alone makes me seem like part of a pair,
without my other half, but that's not true.

I feel grateful to do whatever I want,
to have time to myself,
and care for me.

I'm grateful that I know what love feels like
enough to know I miss it, in a healthy way.

I'm grateful to have the time and space
to get to know and love me,
and to grow.

Happy

Imagine coming out of the bedroom,
to see me with a neon pink poster board
writing with a GIANT sharpie,
making that screeching noise they always do.

H-A-P-P-Y
“I didn’t wake you, did I?”
It was going to be followed by
“birthday” and the girl’s name.

She can’t even answer right away,
the irony catches her off guard,
and she starts to laugh.

She felt anything but happy in that moment,
but still couldn’t pass up the opportunity
to let it make her smile.

Zombie buys glow sticks

When I'm rocking the vampire schedule,
sleeping during the day, and working at night,
I don't feel fully there, cognitively or otherwise.

More of a meat sack shell of a human,
bumbling around, doing my best.
Sometimes I can't even remember
where my car is parked.

But life must go on,
glow sticks must be bought for Halloween parties.

So onward we wander,
half alive, mostly just wanting more sleep,
and rocking whatever brain cells we can muster,
of our own that is.

Wet blanket

I used to say "as exciting as wet cardboard"
but a blanket is much more immersive.

I imagine all their boringness
wrapped around me
cold, wet and miserable.

I can feel them starting to put it around me
on first dates, at work, on transit...
and I'm learning to get up and walk away.

No offense to them,
they be all of that, and all the power to them!
Over there.

Doggy nicknames

You are Happy Tails
when you're excited
and your tail starts knocking things
off every surface low enough.

You are Turd Burglar
when you steal the poop
out of the cat litter box
like it's an expensive hors 'dourve.

You are Raptor Claw
when your paw with the wonky toe
sticks out all funny,
and the nail grows too long.

You are Moochie Poochie
when we're eating,
and you sit at our feet so pretty
with those big eyes.

You are Poop Protestor
when you don't go at all for days
save it all up for us,
and then unleash it in a flurry of farts.

Big spoon, small heartbeat

My dog likes to snuggle, but on her own terms.
She wants all the pets, rolls into you on her back,
but usually prefers her own space to sleep.

Recently she got shaved at the groomers though,
and the temperatures have already dropped,
so she's shivering, and making some big exceptions.

The other day she crawled under the duvet,
and pressed her little furry body into mine
to steal my warmth.

She fell fast asleep, and I could feel her little heart,
pounding away on my arm,
and I fell even more in love with her.

Her soul

She told us she'd give up her soul
for a peppermint brownie cake pop.

If I accepted your soul as payment,
for skippin' you the cake pop,
I'd only want it for a short time,
to nurse it back to healthy, happy and thriving.

And then I'd give it back, all healed
and full of minty brownie cake.

Poster plant for perseverance

At the intersection's corner,
growing right out of the split of concrete
is a wee green plant.

No one told this plant about forests
or fields, or green houses.

They're just doing their best with what they were given,
which was the will to grow, regardless.

I pass this plant often now,
and admire its adversity every single time.

No one's likely told them how great they are though,
until I came along. Groweth upward wee one!

Credit card cake

Without the house keys,
my mom, sister and I
were stuck in the garage.

I so rarely felt like we had time together like that
but we had no choice that day.

Mom opened the extra fridge,
and asked us if we wanted leftover birthday cake for dinner?

I remember her cutting the Costco slab cake
with a Sears credit card from her wallet
and us getting to eat it with our hands.

We laughed together,
and huddled to stay warm.

I felt so loved that day,
I didn't mind so much being locked out of the house.

Fleecy snow

I've always loved how quiet everything gets
when it snows outside.

Science might say it's sound buffering,
or less activity due to the road conditions,
but it's just so peaceful.

Even heavy snow piling up,
has such a serene feeling to it,
despite the chaos it causes.

What I didn't realize until I passed a place
actively doing laundry,
is how fitting the smell of clean dryer smell
fits the whole atmosphere.

It's the added sensory sprinkling
you never knew you needed.

Next time it starts snowing,
grab for the dryer sheets!

Cream cheese commodore

I hadn't been camping with my sister in 20 years
when we traveled down the Oregon Coast together.

So much about us had changed in that time
all the life experiences we collected like beach rocks.

At one of the continental breakfasts on the way down,
I didn't finish everything I grabbed, but didn't want to waste it
so I pocketed a plastic pack of Philadelphia cream cheese.

When we walked away, she started hysterically laughing,
and pulled an identical one of her pocket.

So maybe we've grown,
but deep down we're still so very Dad.

Star chasers

The light screeched so suddenly across the sky,
which was otherwise dead black.

It startled me, but I couldn't react
driving my sister's SUV on a gravel road at 1am
with trees and forest on both sides.

"Did you see that shooting star?"
Oh is that what that was?
How could I miss it, it lit up the whole sky like lightning!

"Make a wish!" And I did.
But maybe its already come true
with 10km runs at night, silent spas
and laughing about all the men we met online in between.

Real happy

He waited in the designated pick-up zone,
at the Kelowna Airport for me. It was only 3 weeks apart,
but we both struggled in our own ways.

I'll never forget how his whole face lit up into the biggest smile,
when he saw me. He wore a button up shirt.
When we first got in the car, he handed me a cute little gift,
and he even put it in a pink gift bag.
He smelled so good, freshly showered and shaved.
I kept nuzzling the soft part of his neck while he drove.

A core memory will stick with me when he wrapped me in a huge hug,
and whispered in my ear, "Is this real?"

Ridiculous malarkey

Wanna run 10km in the dark,
drive to Whistler in the middle of the night,
sleep on a blow-up mattress in my car,
and go to the silent spa the next day?

Sure, what time?

Wanna drive up to Kelowna,
go to two dance shows back-to-back,
fuel ourselves on candy,
and go straight to hockey playoffs?

Sure, what can I bring?

Wanna stop at the cute thrift store,
the day after that wedding you're a bridesmaid in,
despite being sick with a cold,
on our way to a fitness competition?

Sure, why not?

Wanna stay up all night at a Shrek rave,
after working all day in people's mouths,
get up early to eat McDonalds,
and go to Dodgeball playoffs the next day?

Sure, where will we park?

How could any of THAT go sideways?

I get by with a little help from my friends

#GirlGang
We supported each other through pandemic lockdowns,
and all the ups and downs since then.

#GymBros
Two married guys I used to work with,
and work out with at the gym after shifts together.

#CookieCrew
My sister and two dance girlies who motivate each others' fit-
ness
but also bring the candy and cookies.

#Curvies
My hockey team, who took me on as a new player,
and always cheer me on, even when I make mistakes.

#JudoDads
The middle-aged men at my club,
who trained me to be better, without judgement.

#Tea&BookPeople
Wifey, her sisters and their friends who I camp with every year,
a weekend full of reading and drinking tea .

#CuteLittleCult
Mend and another mom I met doing through work,
who've always got advice, and empowering stories.

#SassySquad
Two married women I go to Harrison with every year,
who helped me with online dating, while soaking in the hot springs.

#AMAZEBALLS
My dodgeball team, ever changing in players,
but the energy and solid sportsmanship always stays.

#BookishBabes
A combination of women from all walks of my life,
but we read the same romantasy novels.

Sleepy CJ

I tucked wee T into his bottom bunk bed,
snuggling in with him to read a bedtime story.
I must have fallen asleep first though,
because I woke up with a giant knotted mess on my head.
I wonder if the toddler played with my hair,
attempting to wake me back up.

L was older and orchestrated getting free time,
as he tucked me into the couch with blankets and pillows.
He puts a movie on for us to watch, but I didn't make it through
the opening credits. They did whatever they wanted,
until I woke up 15 minutes before their parents came home.
The sneaky buggers.

Ghost's driving

After another graveyard shift,
when brain activity is at an all-time low,
I stopped at the bank to deposit a cheque
like we're still in the Stone Age!
But a favour for him was worth it.

I went to drive the two blocks home,
but I walked up to the passenger side of the car.

I didn't get in and wait to be driven.
I would have been waiting a while.

Who did I think was going to drive me home?

Dad-less

It felt so wrong, to write a whole book of poetry,
without a single poem about you.

But then I looked back over them,
and realized you're woven in there,
ever present like an undercurrent in my life.

Whenever I have a hard time letting go
of something physical of yours,
I just remember I'm genetically made-up of half of you.

I couldn't write poetry without you in them,
and haven't even today on the 10th anniversary of your passing.

I'll release this near my birthday,
celebrate life, instead of grieving your being gone.

Acknowledgements

This book wouldn't be here without my coworker Megan inspiring me to finally put the poems together, and Wifey (Sarah Neeson) for helping me edit, do the cover art, and publish it.

Countless other people contributed to the experiences these are written about, and many will find themselves in these pages. Thank you the family I'm related to, and my chosen family. Thank you to both my sisters, and Auntie for always believing in me, so wholeheartedly. It's okay Cindy, you don't have to like any of these. Thank you Neeners, my kindered spirit, for inspiring me everyday.

I need to acknowledge all the weirdos out there who are trying to dull their sparkle, and told they're "too much". Those aren't your people, tell them to go find less, and hold out. When you find people who love you for who you are, and feel comfortable being your authentic self, it's a beautiful, magical thing. And then remember to turn around, and help the next weirdo along with their journey. Thank you to my tribe of fellow weirdos, and to you readers, I appreciate every single one of you.

www.ingramcontent.com/pod-product-compliance
Lightning Source LLC
LaVergne TN
LVHW041254150826
845673LV00008B/2588

9781068878206